A TIME TO HEAL

HELD BY HOPE, LIFTED BY LOVE

LITNEY GRAY

DIVINE Flow PUBLISHING

A Collection of Poetry

A TIME TO HEAL

Held by Hope, Lifted by Love

Litney Gray

TESTIMONIALS

"What an amazing collection of poems that speaks for every heart that has been wounded and struggling with despair and unbelief. The words captured the conflicts of the human spirit and societal ills, while never letting go of the truth of God's saving grace and our ability to heal. Each poem left me in awe at the way Litney captured the deep emotions and feelings I am sure many have felt. As hard as I tried to choose a favorite, I was not able to, due to the beauty of them all!"

Dr. Julie Gray, PsyD, LCSW Founder and Lead Clinician of Dr. Julie Gray Lighted Pathways Psychology Inc.

Author of Diva Five Alive Aunt

"This collection of poems is poignant and timely, eliciting emotions and memories with each reading. Litney is truly talented compiling relatable and relevant writings that are both comforting and thought-provoking."

Dr. William Johnson, M.D

Uncle

"Whether poetry, podcast or ministry, you spit fire, Sis! Your poems are so refreshing, inspiring and timely. Thank you for being a willing vessel, it's an honor to call you sister/friend."

Meissa Releford

Minister Sister/Friend

To my parents, Vincent & Leona Gray, as we have walked this time by faith. To my sisters, Leontae', Vinchessica and VinSche', we have come this far by faith. To all my family, friends, church family, communities and the readers of this book, I hope you are encouraged to keep living and move ahead with Light not just at the end of the tunnel but through it with these words from...

"A Time to Heal"

CONTENTS

IN LOVING MEMORY

To my grandmother, Lena Gray, I miss your pretty face, but I thank God for the time we spent together. To my grandfather, Oliver Gray Jr. and great-uncle, Eddie Gray for always supporting me. You remain a big part of this journey.

I love you all always.

To those loved ones who have taken their eternal rest, your presence is dearly missed, but your love remains present.

NOTE TO READER

I have learned many lessons about embracing the purpose of life given our time-sensitive existence. I have experienced these lessons at various times and seasons of my life. In the year of 2020, the onset of a global deadly pandemic, political unrest and social tension amplified the reminder that life is short. Pain, sorrow, loss, death and grief are not biased, hold no political interest, are never concerned about socioeconomic status, and cannot be coerced by one's charm and beauty. Both young and old can experience their 3-D effect on the body, soul and spirit. You too, may have your own recollection of life experiences and lessons. I do not aim to compare whose experiences are lesser or greater because our lives are respectfully unique.

In light of the discomfort of experiences, where does one find hope to heal? Where does courage and hope come from to face another day?

*As you read these poems, be comforted in the embrace of Hope. Time is being allowed to mend, stitch and cure. Time has been allowed to heal the brokenhearted. Whether you take one day or one month to read this book, just keep going, following Hope, and experience that there is Light for you. Through these pages, may Hope relieve and revive you as you read, "**A Time to Heal**."*

ONE
HELD

Hurt, but can't feel.

Numbness.

Words within, but can't speak.

Dumbness.

Thinking thoughts, but not thinking.

Dazed.

Pause. Rewind. Play. Retake.

Can anyone make the shock of this pain go away?

Speaking to God without vocal cords.

Heart muttering some kind of plea to the Lord. His words faintly heard, but sure.

His words are softly spoken, but pure.

Eyes full of tears.

Mind clouded with fears. Knees too weak to stand. Collapsing,

falling,

gasping for air,

letting out that cry,

but suddenly, held. Suddenly,

Held by Hope,

for purpose,

only time will tell.

TWO
THE CHILDREN ARE CRYING

The children are crying

Daughters and sons alike

The children are crying

Death and grief trouble their spirits at night

The children are crying

Their tears flow like the abundance of rain

The children are crying

They search for an explanation to this pain

The children are crying

Has anyone cared to understand their heart's condition?

The children are crying

Will anyone relieve their emotional affliction?

The children are crying

Men and women to be

The children are crying

Death and grief trouble their outlook of destiny

The children are crying

Their dreams halted during this space and time

The children are crying,

Their faith and hope confined

Whose children are crying, the children of young or old?

All these children are crying; for grief left time untold.

Dear God, please hear the cry of the children; please, dear LORD, see their tears.

Our Father, in heaven, comfort their hearts; LORD deliver them from all their fears.

A Time to Heal

You can choose to do one or
more of the following now:
Pause
Ponder
Pray
Sing
Write
Draw
Breathe

THREE
THE DAY JESUS WEPT

Nothing caught him by surprise,

Yet teardrops formed in his eyes.

A friend lost had many grieving.

Faith stretched left some unbelieving…

The day Jesus wept.

Though he knew he was just asleep,

This moment declared a time to weep.

Weeping was the only action

That could express the moans and groans of his compassion.

For his presence was not welcomed with satisfaction

The day Jesus wept.

Couldn't he have avoided the dismay? Couldn't he have intervened before disarray? Why now, would we give thought to pray...

The day Jesus wept.

The day Jesus wept was not meant to mark the end of hope for eternal life. For his Spirit declared he was God, yet his humanity reminded him that he was the Christ.

Thus, he would even have to bear this grief to Calvary to offer the perfect sacrifice.

So the day he wept the heavens seemed still

To consider His divine purpose and will,

To ponder how a great God could feel,

To understand that His love is real;

For his tears watered the seed of hope for His glory to be revealed.

FOUR
THE LOVE OF GOD

Love is enduring, more solid than gold.

Love is strong, never waxing old.

Love is tough, not easily-broken.

Love is always present, even though seemingly stolen.

What manner of love will mend broken hearts?

What manner of love can hold together what seems to have fallen apart?

What manner of love will comfort the sorrow-filled eyes?

What manner of love can explain the what now and why?

The love of the Savior will mend.

The love of a Friend can hold.

The love of the Father will comfort.

The love of God can send peace to the story yet to unfold.

FIVE
WILL GOD HEAL IN THIS PLACE?

Will God heal in this place, where sorrow and pain abide?

Can God heal in this place, where silent tears are cried?

Does God heal in this place, where comfort comes and goes?

Why God, this place, is what I want to know?!

I will heal in this place, for I AM the God that healeth thee.

I can heal in this place, for there's nothing too hard for ME.

I do heal in this place, for I AM come that you might have life and that more abundantly.

SIX
JOY

Joy is here with strength holding me together.

Though facing trials and tribulation, I am assured things will get better.

Joy did not shun pain or tears.

It courageously pressed on, overcoming the fears.

Though weeping was permitted to endure for a night,

Joy kept coming in the morning with the Light.

The oil of joy for mourning overflowed.

Happiness was a byproduct of a joyful soul.

Joy interrupted the sorrowful song,

Reviving life to chords that seemed down for so long.

Joy was so excited it leapt ahead,

Teaching feet to learn to keep going and dance.

SEVEN
THE ROAD TO RECOVERY

What if it hurts;

What if it bends?

What if it's the start;

What if it's the end?

What if it breaks;

What if it bleeds?

How long will it take to repair the breach?

What if it burns;

What if it smells?

What if life's troubles swell?

What if it stings;

What if it's sore?

What if I settle here, though I dreamed for more?

27

What if I let go;

What if I hold on?

Will I ever find the strength to carry on?

What if I'm restless;

What if it's hard for me to keep still?

What if I must recognize ...

It's a time to heal.

What if I choose life;

What if I choose to live?

What if I choose to get what I have desired to give?

What if I choose purpose;

What if I choose time?

What if I choose the future from the thoughts of God's mind.

EIGHT
LIFE IS A GIFT

Life is a gift, so precious, so fragile.

With love, tender care and prayer, it must be handled.

Precious memories, moments and meetings captured in time.

No auditions or rewind.

Life is a gift to cherish, to love and live.

Life is a gift with purpose that God gives.

Live

NINE
LOOK UP

Up from the ashes

Up from the ground

Up from the grave

Life yet abounds

Up from despair

Up from disbelief

Up from the sorrows

There is relief

Up from the hurt

Up from the pain

Up from disappointments

Here is the exchange

Beauty for ashes

The oil of joy for mourning

A garment of praise for heaviness

To embrace a new dawning

Look up and listen

Get up and see

Look up and live

There is time to redeem.

TEN
A TIME TO HEAL

Two hands on a clock and two hands in the sky
Telling time to explain life's who, what, when
and why.

Every tick and tock hold a loss.

While the sun and moon add up the cost:

- The cost of time halted by grief and sadness
- The cost of time stolen by fear and madness
- The weight of time lost and gained,

Trying hearts overwhelmed and strained,

As they bear yesterday's frustration and fear
tomorrow's pain.

Though the shorthand forecasts sunshine, the
longhand forecasts rain.

The future looks bright, but the present is too cloudy to predict such hope.

The hour declares a time to heal, while the minute a time to choke.

Each second simultaneously holds two wills.

Though the pressures of life edge a time to kill,

Thank God for this moment, that is, *A TIME TO HEAL*.

AUTHOR'S REFLECTION

'Tis this moment to reflect,

On the blessings of life in spite of its tests.

We have survived, some even thrived, many are still holding on despite the tears in their eyes.

'Tis a time to weep and a time to laugh,

A time to be grateful for what we can give and what we have.

'Tis this moment we gather to share what has been given, Spreading life through these experiences that we are living.

'Tis the day to appreciate, though the night may seem cold. We are still here as time unfolds.

Joy bells may fade in the background of emergency sirens, yet we anticipate a better horizon.

'Tis the hour to feel the heat of Hope. Here is a moment to heal and to cope.

For some the days and nights seem uniquely quiet.

Still, I have known healing to emerge out of the silence.

Now, even on the busiest of days, may peace come through life's highs and lows. And even in the darkest of nights, let love shine bright -let it glow, let it glow, let it glow.

No matter how near and no matter how far.

May goodness, comfort and grace find you wherever you are.

'Tis these poems, I reflect:

I am so thankful for life and for that, I am blessed.

ACKNOWLEDGMENTS

I want to thank my Lord and Savior Jesus Christ. God, I give you all the glory for the gifts you placed inside of me to serve others. Thank You for inspiring timely words in this journey of life.

Thank you dad and mom, Vincent and Leona Gray. I am ever grateful for your loving support, encouragement and certainly your prayers. Dad, God has used your godly admonition, and Mom, your writer's wit in developing my unique pen. To my three older sisters, Leontae', Vinchessica and VinSche', thanks for always loving and supporting your baby sister. Dominic, Azariah and Ezra, may you always know God cares about you and loves you so much. Thank you grandparents, Leon and Carrie Good, for your love and care for so many, but especially towards me. I pray God's salvation, comfort, healing and peace be your portion. To my immediate and extended family and friends, teachers, school faculty and staff, colleagues and the communities that I have been blessed to be a part of, I pray that the God of peace will sustain you through every time and season of your life.

Special thanks to Christian Joy Wagner and Camelle ilona for your support of this book of poetry. Special thanks to the generous women of P:31 for your overwhelming support and investment. To the Divine Flow Publishing Editorial team, Kimberley Lawson, Jeanette McCarthy, and Peter Daley, thank you for working with me. To my aunt, Dr. Thrisha Shiver, you are an answer to prayer in sharpening me with your expertise. Thank you!

Thank you to Bishop A. Glenn Brady, First Lady Angela Brady and the New Bethel Church family, I thank God for you. To the church ministries and caring individuals who have poured into my life, hope and the word of God, I thank you all for your encouragement and prayers.

APPENDICES

Book Cover Design:
Will L. Lewis IV
www.wlewisiv.com

Dr. Julie Gray, PsyD, LCSW
Founder and Lead Clinician of Dr. Julie Gray Lighted
Pathways Psychology Inc.
Author of Diva Five Alive
www.lightedpathways.org

GRAYT SOLUTIONS LLC, Consulting
www.graytsolutions.com

Camelle ilona
of the House of ilona
www.linktr.ee/Camelleilona

ABOUT THE AUTHOR

Litney is a native of Gary, Indiana. She is a messenger of encouragement and inspiration who shares timely and purposeful poetry. She inspires, ignites, and impacts with a voice of hope, faith, and love.

Visit: www.litneylynn.com

MORE FROM THE AUTHOR

Poems for Special Occasions at <u>www.litneylynn.com</u>

CHARITY

Grace Beyond Borders NWI, Inc., was founded in 2013 by
Marcus Martin as a non-profit organization with the
purpose of meeting the physical and spiritual needs of
those impacted by homelessness and drug addiction.
Thanks to established partnerships and donations from
individuals, churches, organizations, and agencies in the
community, our staff, and volunteers are able to provide
food, clothing, and referrals for lodging to those in need.
God is using Grace Beyond Borders NWI, Inc to change
the lives of men, women, and children in desperate need.
Donate and learn more at

www.gracebeyondborders.org

www.ingramcontent.com/pod-product-compliance
Lightning Source LLC
LaVergne TN
LVHW051818080426
835513LV00017B/2007

* 9 7 8 0 5 7 8 9 4 1 7 2 1 *